Jazzin' About Styles

Easy fun pieces for piano/keyboard

Leichte und fetzige Stücke für Klavier/Keyboard

Morceaux faciles et divertissants pour piano our clavier

Pamela Wedgwood

CONTENTS

© 1996 by Faber Music Ltd
First published in 1996 by Faber Music Ltd
3 Queen Square London WC1N 3AU
Music engraved by Wessex Music Services
Printed in England by Halstan & Co Ltd

ISBN 0 571 51718 8

FABER *ff* MUSIC

Play that Banjo!

Style: Dixieland
Emerged from the southern states of America and Dixie bands almost always included a banjo. Make the music bounce.

Style: Dixieland
Originaires des Etats du Sud de l'Amérique, les orchestres Dixie comprenaient presque toujours un banjo. C'est une musique pleine de verve.

Im Stil des Dixieland
Diese Musik stammt aus den Südstaaten der USA, wo in den entsprechenden Ensembles fast immer ein Banjo mitspielte. Die Musik soll tanzen und springen.

Big-Band Boogie

Style: Swing tempo with an easy boogie bass.
In the mid-thirties Boogie Woogie exploded onto the jazz scene. The boogie beat contains a repeating left- hand pattern. Both Count Basie and Fats Waller played in this style.

Style: Tempo de swing avec basse boogie nonchalante.
Au milieu des années trente, le Boogie Woogie prit d'assaut les scènes de jazz. Le style boogie renferme une figure continue à la main gauche. Count Basie et Fats Waller jouèrent tous deux dans ce style.

Stil: im Swing-Tempo mit einem leichten Boogie-Baß
In der Mitte der 30er Jahre dieses Jahrhunderts eroberte der Boogie Woogie die Jazz-Szene. Im Boogie gibt es eine ständig wiederholte Figur in der linken Hand. Sowohl Count Basie als auch Fats Waller musizierten in diesem Stil.

Contra-Flow!

Style: Moderate Swing (using a walking bass).
Your left hand is a double bass! Your right hand is the swing band accompanying!

Style: swing modéré (avec "walking bass").
Votre main gauche est une contrebasse! Votre main droite est l'orchestre de swing qui l'accompagne!

Im Stil eines mäßign Swing (mit durchlaufender Baßfigur).
Die linke Hand spielt eine Kontrabass-Stimme, die rechte Hand entspricht der begleitenden Swing-Band.

St. George and the Dragon

Style: Heavy metal
This music is usually played on electric guitars and is a very aggressive rock style. If you have different sounds on your keyboard experiment with them!

Style: Heavy metal
Cette musique est généralement jouée sur des guitares électriques dans un style rock très agressif. Si vous avez des sons différents sur votre clavier, c'est l'occasion ou jamais de les essayer!

Im Stil von Heavy Metal
Diese Musik wird normalerweise auf elektrischen Gitarren gespielt; es handelt sich um einen sehr aggressiven Rock. Wenn auf dem Keyboard verschiedene sounds möglich sind, sollte damit experimentiert werden.

Up and Away!

Style: Jazz waltz
Play the right-hand dotted rhythms in a very relaxed way, make them sound almost like a triplet.

Style: Jazz waltz
Jouez les rythmes pointés de la main droite d'une manière très détendue, faites-les presque ressembler à un triolet.

Im Stil eines Jazz-Walzers
Die punktierten Rhythmen der linken Hand sollen locker und entspannt gespielt werden, so daß sie fast wie Triolen klingen.

There ain't no beer in Cow-Horn Creek!

Style: Country blues
Think of those dusty, desert towns in the wild west of America! Play lazily.

Style: Country blues
Songez aux villes poussiéreuses et désertiques du Far-West! Jouez paresseusement.

Im Stil eines ländlichen Blues
Man denke an die staubigen Wüstenstädte im Wilden Westen Amerikas. Das Stück soll bequem und faul klingen!

Easy Life

Style: Slow swing
This piece is written in the style of Glen Miller, the great war-time band-leader. Use your swing setting on the keyboard.

Style: swing lent
Ce morceau est écrit dans le style de Glen Miller, grand chef d'orchestre de variétés pendant la Seconde guerre mondiale. Utilisez le registre "swing" du clavier.

Im Stil eines langsamen Swing
Das Stück ist im Stil Glen Millers komponiert, der während des Zweiten Weltkriegs eine berühmte Band leitete. Auf dem Keyboard die Swing-Einstellung verwenden!

No Fixed Address

Style: Slow blues
Traditionally, the Blues are associated with sadness. Louis Armstrong on trumpet, Lester Young on tenor sax and Charlie Parker on alto sax, were some of the greatest Blues players.

Style: blues lent
Le blues est synonyme de tristesse. Louis Armstrong à la trompette, Lester Young au saxophone ténor et Charlie Parker au saxophone alto comptèrent parmi les plus grand interprètes de blues.

Im Stil eines langsamen Blues
Der Blues wird traditionell mit Traurigkeit assoziiert. Louis Armstrong (Trompete), Lester Young (Tenorsaxophon) und Charlie Parker (Altsaxophon) gehörten zu den berühmtesten Blues-Spielern.

Cuba-Libre!

Style: Lively rhumba
The Rhumba is of Cuban origin and became a popular dance style in the 1930's. Cuba Libre is also a delicious cocktail of rum and coke!

Style: rumba
D'origine cubaine, la rumba devint un style de danse populaire dans les années trente. "Cuba Libre" est aussi un délicieux cocktail de rhum et de coke!

Im Stil einer Rumba
Die Rumba stammt aus Kuba und war in den 30er Jahren dieses Jahrhunderts ein beliebter Tanz. Cuba Libre ist auch der Name eines köstlichen Mixgetränks aus Rum und Cola.

Shoe-Shine Rag

Style: Ragtime
Introduced to America by African slaves. In the late 1800's a craze for a new kind of music called Ragtime swept America. Ragtime makes use of syncopation (when the accent appears on an irregular beat). Scott Joplin contributed many Ragtime pieces to the repertoire including 'The Entertainer'. Don't play this too fast!

Style: ragtime
Introduit en Amérique par les esclaves africains. A la fin du dix-neuvième siècle, l'Amérique s'enthousiasma pour ce nouveau genre musical. Le ragtime utilise la syncope (qui place l'accent rythmique sur un temps irrégulier). Scott Joplin a écrit de nombreux morceaux de ragtime, dont "The Entertainer". Ne jouez pas ce morceau trop vite!

Im Stil des ursprünglichen Ragtime
Der Ragtime wurde durch afrikanische Sklaven nach Amerika eingeführt und verbreitete sich dort gegen Ende des 19. Jahrhunderts mit unglaublichem Tempo. Der Ragtime lebt von Synkopierungen (d.h., daß eine eigentlich schwache Zählzeit betont wird). Scott Joplin erweiterte das Ragtime-Repertoire um viele Stücke, darunter auch den "Entertainer". Nicht zu schnell spielen!

Wanted

Style: Hard rock
Uses a very strong slowish beat with stresses on the 2nd and 4th beat of each bar.

Style: Hard rock
Emploie un rythme très puissant et plutôt lent avec des accents sur les deuxième et quatrième temps forts de chaque mesure.

Im Stil des Hard Rock
Ein sehr kräftiger, langsamer beat mit Betonungen auf der zweiten und vierten Zählzeit jeden Taktes.

On the Rocks!

Style: Rock 'n' roll
Rock 'n' Roll made a dramatic appearance during the 1950's. It is usually played energetically and at a fairly fast tempo.

Style: Rock 'n' Roll
Le Rock 'n' Roll fit une apparition spectaculaire durant les années cinquante. Il est généralement joué d'une manière énergique et sur un rythme assez rapide.

Im Stil des Rock 'n' Roll
Der Rock 'n' Roll war während der 50er Jahre unglaublich beliebt. Er wird meist energisch und in ziemlich schnellem Tempo gespielt.

Street Place

Style: Romantic piano
Lots of musical expression is needed to shape a piece like this. Think about the tempo, volume and phrasing and use both pedals.

Style: piano romantique
Une grande expression musicale est nécessaire pour donner corps à un morceau comme celui-ci. Songez au tempo, au volume et au phrasé, et utilisez les deux pédales.

Stil: Romantisches Klavierstück
Das Stück verlangt viel musikalischen Ausdruck. Man achte auf Tempo, Klang und Phrasierung und verwende beide Pedale.

New World

Style: Free expression
Think of this music describing a scene from a film. Play very deliberately and make full use of your pedal.

Style: expression libre
Imaginez que cette musique décrit une scène de film. Jouez très posément et utilisez souvent la pédale.

Stil: Frei im Ausdruck
Man spiele diese Musik so, als ob sie die Vertonung einer Filmszene sei. Sehr ausdrucksvoll und mit viel Pedal spielen.

Chocolate Car-Park

Style: Disco
A very lively dance beat which is always kept at the same tempo. If you have a disco beat on your keyboard play along with it!

Style: disco
Un rythme de danse très animé et très régulier. C'est le moment d'employer le registre disco de votre clavier!

Im Disco-Stil
Der sehr lebhafte Tanzrhythmus wird im gleichen Tempo durchgehalten. Wenn es auf dem Keyboard einen Disco- Rhythmus gibt, kann er hier eingesetzt werden.

Homeward Bound

Style: Pop ballad
A strong melodic line, characteristically slow and stylish.

Style: Pop ballad
Une ligne mélodique puissante, typiquement lente et gracieuse.

Im Stil einer Pop-Ballade
Melodisch ausdrucksvoll, auf charakteristische Weise langsam und elegant.

4

Style: Dixieland

Play that Banjo!

Style: Swing

Big-Band Boogie

In swing tempo (♩ = c. 112)

Style: Walking bass

Contra-Flow!

With a good swing (♩ = c. 116)

Style: Heavy metal

St. George and the Dragon

Rough and ready with a strong beat (♩ = c. 120)

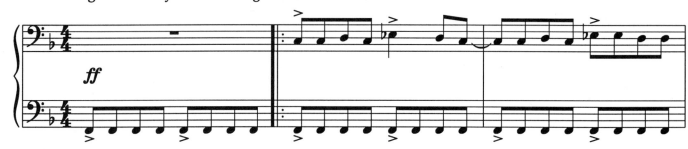

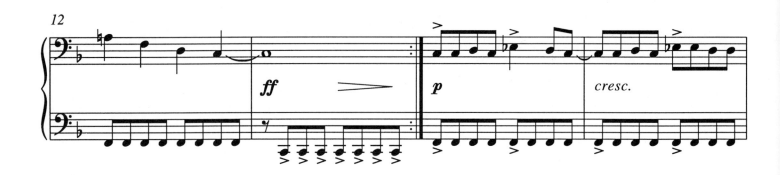

Style: Jazz waltz.

Up and Away!

With hot air (♩ = c. 112)

Style: Country blues

There ain't no beer in Cow-Horn Creek!

With a sober beat! (♩. = c. 72-80)

NO   BEER!

Style: Slow swing (Glen Miller)

Easy Life

Style: Slow blues

No Fixed Address

Style: Lively rhumba

Cuba-Libre!

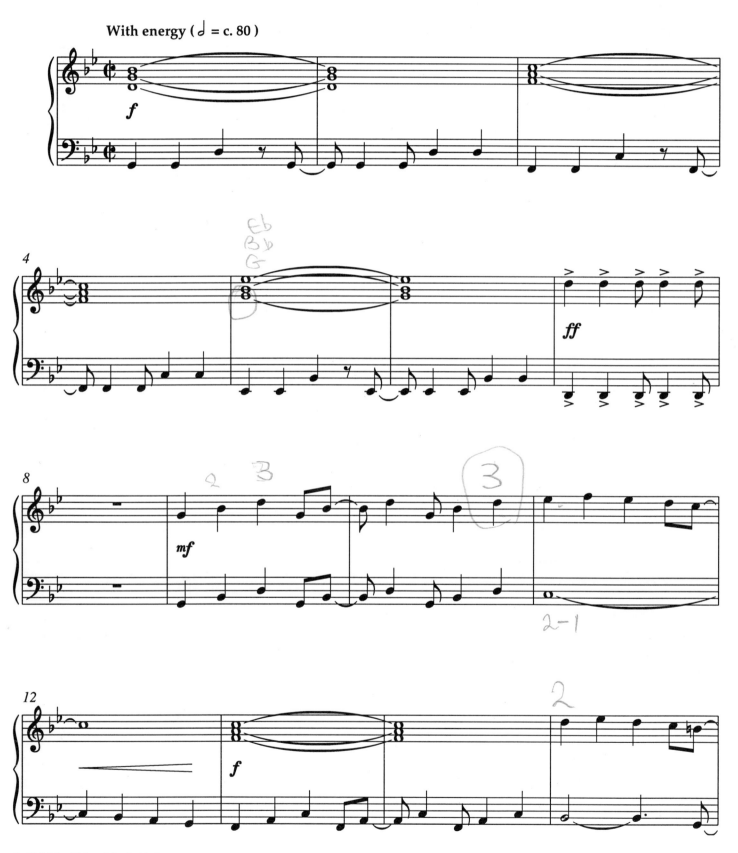

Style: Ragtime

Shoe-Shine Rag

In moderate Rag time (♩ = c. 112)

Style: Hard rock

Wanted

Style: Rock 'n' roll

On the Rocks!

Style: Romantic piano

Street Place

With feeling (♩ = c. 92)

Style: Free expression

New World

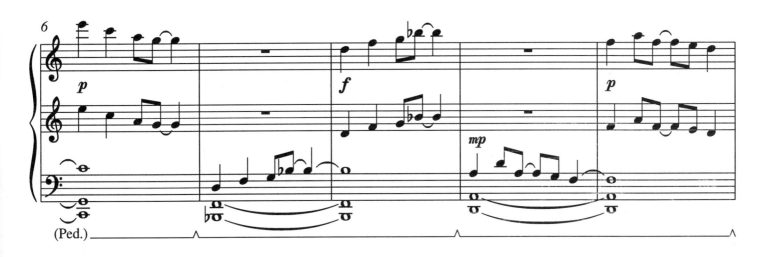

Style: Disco

Chocolate Car-Park

to Judy

With a lively disco beat (♩ = c. 112)

© 1996 by Faber Music Ltd.

Style: Pop ballad

Homeward Bound

Peacefully (♩. = c. 56)